Stunnir

MW00916250

Easy Friendship Bracelet Patterns

Young Curry

Table of Contents

Chapter One

Friendship Bracelets

Friendship bracelets are not just colorful bands adorning the wrist; they are a symbol of connection, affection and lasting friendship. From simple designs to intricate designs, each bracelet carries the essence of shared memories and moments. In this book, we take a journey through the art of making friendship bracelets, exploring different patterns that reflect the beauty of friendship and the joy of creating together.

Getting Started

Making friendship bracelets is a wonderful craft that only requires a few basic materials and a dash of creativity. We cover everything you need to start your journey into the world of knotting and weaving friendship bracelets.

Materials needed:

1. Embroidery thread is the basic material for crafting friendship bracelets. It comes in a wide range of colors and is usually made of cotton or silk. Choose your favorite colors or opt for a rainbow assortment to create vibrant patterns.

2. Scissors: A good pair of sharp scissors is essential to cut the embroidery thread to the desired length. Make sure they are comfortable to hold and can easily cut through several strands of thread.

3. Clipboard or tape: To keep the bracelet stable as you work, you'll need something to anchor it in place. A clipboard works well, but if you don't have one, you can tape the bracelet to a flat surface like a desk or table.

4. Optional: Beads and charms: Beads and charms are not necessary to make basic bracelets, but they can add extra

flair and personalization to your creations. Choose beads in a variety of shapes and sizes to complement your designs.

Knotting Techniques:

Before diving into bracelet patterns, it is essential that you familiarize yourself with a few basic knotting techniques:

1. Forward Knot (FK): To create a forward knot, take the left strand and cross it over the middle strands, creating a "4" shape. Then pass it under the right strand and pull it through the hole and tighten the knot. Repeat this process with the right strand.

2. Backward Knot (BK): A back knot is basically the opposite of a front knot. Start by taking the right strand and crossing it over the middle strands, creating a backwards "4" shape. Loop it under the left strand and pull it through the hole and tighten the knot. Repeat with the left strand.

3. Combination Knots: Many friendship bracelet designs include a combination of forward and reverse knots to create intricate designs. Practice alternating these two knots to master more complex patterns.

Tips for beginners:

Start with simple patterns: Start with simple patterns that use only a few colors and basic knotting techniques. As you gain confidence, you can gradually tackle more complex patterns.

Keep your knots tight: To ensure a neat and uniform bracelet, make sure you tighten each knot securely as you work.

Experiment with colors: Don't be afraid to combine colors to create unique combinations. The beauty of friendship bracelets lies in their endless possibilities for creativity.

Chapter Two

Simple Beginnings

Let's start with the basics, exploring simple friendship bracelet designs that are perfect for beginners. These patterns focus on mastering basic knotting techniques to create elegant and understated patterns. Let's dive in and start our journey into the world of friendship bracelet making.

1. Single Color Bracelets:

Single color bracelets are a great starting point for beginners. They allow you to focus on mastering basic knotting techniques without the added complexity of multiple colors.

Pattern: Basic Stripes

Materials needed: One skein of embroidery thread in the desired color, scissors, clipboard or tape.

Instructions:

1. Cut a piece of embroidery thread approximately 60 inches long.

2. Fold the thread in half and tie a knot at the top, leaving a loop for attaching the bracelet later.

3. Tape the loop to the clipboard or surface.

4. Divide the thread into two equal halves with three strands in each half.

5. Take the leftmost strand and make forward knots on adjacent strands until it reaches the center.

6. Repeat the same process with the rightmost strand, making front knots on adjacent strands until it touches the center.

7. Continue knotting in this manner, alternating between the left and right strands, until the bracelet reaches the desired length.

8. Once you reach the end, tie a knot to tie the strands together, leaving a small loop for fastening.

2. Two-Color Stripes:

Once you're happy with single-color bracelets, you can experiment with a two-color design to add variety and visual interest to your creations.

Pattern: Alternating Stripes

Materials needed: Two skeins of embroidery thread in contrasting colors, scissors, clipboard or tape.

Instructions:

1. Cut a piece of embroidery thread from each color about 60 inches long.

2. Fold the strands in half and tie a knot at the top, leaving a loop for fastening.

3. Tape the loop to the clipboard or surface.

4. Arrange the strands so that you have two sets of three strands, one color in each set.

5. Take the leftmost strand from the first set and make forward knots on the adjacent strands until it reaches the center.

6. Repeat the same process with the leftmost strand from the second set, creating front knots on adjacent strands until it touches the center.

7. Continue alternating both colors and making forward knots until the bracelet reaches the desired length.

8. At the end, tie a knot to connect the strands, leaving a small loop for fastening.

Exploratory Patterns

Now that you've mastered the basics, it's time to explore different friendship bracelet designs. Here we delve into more complex designs that showcase the versatility and creativity of knotting techniques. Get ready to hone your bracelet making skills and create stunning pieces that reflect the beauty of friendship.

1. Chevron Friendship Bracelet:

The Chevron pattern is a classic design that features zigzag lines. It's a timeless favorite among friendship bracelet enthusiasts and can be customized with a variety of color combinations.

Pattern: Classic Chevron

Materials needed: Several skeins of embroidery thread in the colors of your choice (at least three colors for a bright arrow-shaped effect), scissors, clipboard or tape.

Instructions:

1. Choose three or more colors of embroidery thread for your bracelet.

2. Cut strands of each color approximately 60 inches long.

3. Fold the strands in half and tie a knot at the top, leaving a loop for fastening.

4. Tape the loop to the clipboard or surface.

5. Arrange the strands so that you have the same number of strands in each color.

6. Take the leftmost strand and make forward knots on adjacent strands until it reaches the center.

7. Repeat the same process with the rightmost strand, creating front knots on adjacent strands until it touches the center.

8. Continue alternating between the left and right strands, creating forward knots to create a V-shaped pattern.

9. Once you have completed the first row, repeat the process, starting from the outer strands and working towards the center.

10. Continue knotting until the bracelet reaches the desired length.

11. At the end, tie a knot to connect the strands, leaving a small loop for fastening.

2. Diamond Friendship Bracelet:

The diamond pattern adds a touch of geometric elegance to your bracelets. It is a versatile design that can be customized with different colors and sizes to suit your preferences.

Pattern: Geometric Diamonds

Materials needed: Multiple skeins of embroidery thread in your desired colors (at least two colors for contrasting diamonds), scissors, clipboard or tape.

Instructions:

1. Choose two contrasting colors of embroidery thread for your bracelet.

2. Cut strands of each color approximately 60 inches long.

3. Fold the strands in half and tie a knot at the top, leaving a loop for fastening.

4. Tape the loop to the clipboard or surface.

5. Arrange the strands so that you have the same number of strands in each color.

6. Take the leftmost strand and make forward knots on adjacent strands until it reaches the center.

7. Repeat the same process with the rightmost strand, creating front knots on adjacent strands until it touches the center.

8. Continue knotting in this manner, alternating between the left and right strands to create diagonal rows of color.

9. Once you've completed the first row, repeat the process, starting from the outermost strands and working towards the center to create more rows of diamonds.

10. Continue knotting until the bracelet reaches the desired length.

11. At the end, tie a knot to connect the strands, leaving a small loop for fastening.

Chapter Three

Friendship in Bloom

We celebrate the beauty of nature by exploring friendship bracelet designs inspired by flowers and other botanical elements. From delicate petals to vibrant blooms, these designs capture the essence of friendship in full bloom. Let's fill our bracelets with the colors and shapes of the natural world as we embark on this floral journey together.

1. Flower Friendship Bracelet:

Embrace the beauty of flowers
with this gorgeous pattern that
incorporates petals and blossoms
into your bracelet design.
Whether you choose a single
flower or a bouquet of flowers,

this pattern is sure to add a touch of charm to your creations.

Pattern: Blooming Petals

Materials needed: Several skeins of embroidery thread in different colors (for petals, stems and leaves), scissors, a clipboard or tape.

Instructions:

1. Choose the colors you want for the petals, stems and leaves. You will need at least three colors for a basic floral design.

2. Cut strands of each color approximately 60 inches long.

3. Fold the strands in half and tie a knot at the top, leaving a loop for fastening.

4. Tape the loop to the clipboard or surface.

5. Start by creating a central floral design. Choose one color for the center of the flower and create a small circle of knots using the knots forward.

6. Choose a different petal color and make loops going outwards around the center circle using front knots.

7. Continue adding petals in a circular pattern until you reach

the desired fullness of your flower.

8. Once the flower is complete, use the green embroidery thread to create the stems and leaves using front knots.

9. Continue knotting in this manner, alternating between petals, stems and leaves, until the bracelet reaches the desired length.

10. At the end, tie a knot to connect the strands, leaving a small loop for fastening.

2. Sunburst Friendship Bracelet:

Radiate warmth and positivity with this solar pattern that captures the radiant energy of the sun. With its bold design and bright colors, this bracelet is sure to put a smile on your face and warm your heart.

Pattern: Sunny Rays

Materials needed: Several skeins of embroidery thread in warm, sunny colors (such as yellow, orange and red), scissors, clipboard or tape.

Instructions:

1. Choose the colors you want for your sunburst design. Warm, sunny colors such as yellow, orange and red work well with this pattern.

2. Cut strands of each color approximately 60 inches long.

3. Fold the strands in half and tie a knot at the top, leaving a loop for fastening.

4. Tape the loop to the clipboard or surface.

5. Begin by creating a central sunburst design. Choose one color for the center of the sun and create a small circle of knots using the knots forward.

6. Choose a different color for the sun rays and create loops pointing outwards around the central circle using forward knots.

7. Continue adding rays in a circular pattern until you reach

the desired fullness for your
sunburst.

8. Once the sunburst is
complete, use alternating colors
to create bands of color around
the sun using forward knots.

9. Continue knotting in this
manner, alternating between
sunbeams and colored bands,
until the bracelet reaches the
desired length.

10. At the end, tie a knot to
connect the strands, leaving a
small loop for fastening.

Advanced Creations

We'll explore friendship bracelet designs that push the boundaries of creativity and skill. These advanced designs incorporate intricate knotting techniques and intricate patterns to create bracelets that are as beautiful as they are challenging. Get ready to take your bracelet making skills to the next level as we embark on this journey of creativity and craftsmanship.

1. Fishtail Friendship Bracelet:

The fishtail pattern is a stunning braided design that adds another layer of complexity to your bracelets. With its intricate weaving and striking structure, this pattern is sure to turn heads.

Pattern: Braided Elegance

Materials needed: Several skeins of embroidery thread in complementary colors, scissors, clipboard or tape.

Instructions:

   1. Choose two or more complementary colors for your fishtail bracelet.

   2. Cut strands of each color approximately 60 inches long.

   3. Fold the strands in half and tie a knot at the top, leaving a loop for fastening.

   4. Tape the loop to the clipboard or surface.

5. Divide the strands into two equal groups, one color in each group.

6. Take the leftmost strand from the first group and make a front knot on the adjacent strand in the second group.

7. Repeat this process with the rightmost strand from the second group and make a front knot on the adjacent strand in the first group.

8. Continue alternating between the left and right strands and create front knots to create a fishtail pattern.

9. When knotted, the strands begin to intertwine and create a beautiful braided effect.

10. Continue knotting until the bracelet reaches the desired length.

11. At the end, tie a knot to connect the strands, leaving a small loop for fastening.

2. Chinese Staircase Friendship Bracelet:

The Chinese staircase pattern is a fascinating design that features intricate loops and knots. Although challenging, the end result is well worth the effort and creates a bracelet that is as stunning as it is unique.

Pattern: Stairway to Friendship

Materials needed: Several skeins of embroidery thread in your desired colors, scissors, clipboard or tape.

Instructions:

1. Choose two or more colors for your Chinese stairs bracelet.

2. Cut strands of each color approximately 60 inches long.

3. Fold the strands in half and tie a knot at the top, leaving a loop for fastening.

4. Tape the loop to the clipboard or surface.

5. Arrange the strands so that you have the same number of strands in each color.

6. Take the leftmost strand and make a front knot on the adjacent strand, pulling it through to form a loop.

7. Repeat this process, creating forward knots and loops around each other as you go.

8. As you continue to knot, the loops will form a staircase-like pattern, hence the name "Chinese Staircase."

9. Continue knotting until the bracelet reaches the desired length.

10. At the end, tie a knot to connect the strands, leaving a small loop for fastening.

Chapter Four

Personalized Touches

Let's explore ways to add unique and personalized touches to your friendship bracelets. From incorporating beads and charms to experimenting with your own designs, these techniques allow you to breathe even more personality and meaning into your creations. Let's dive in and find out how to make each bracelet truly unique.

1. Adding Beads:

Beads are a fantastic way to add texture, color and flair to friendship bracelets. Whether you choose tiny seed beads for subtle detail or larger beads for a bold statement, the possibilities are endless.

Pattern: beaded Accents

Materials needed: Multiple skeins of embroidery thread, various beads in different sizes and colors, beading needle (optional), scissors, clipboard or tape.

Instructions:

1. Choose a bracelet pattern to serve as the basis for your design.

2. When tying the bracelet, periodically thread the beads onto

one or more strands of embroidery thread.

3. You can use a needle to thread the beads onto the thread, especially for smaller beads.

4. Experiment with different bead placements and patterns to create unique patterns.

5. Continue knotting and adding beads until the bracelet is the desired length.

6. At the end, tie a knot to connect the strands, leaving a small loop for fastening.

2. Customization using Charms:

Charms are a charming way to add personalization and symbolism to friendship bracelets. Whether you choose charms that represent shared interests, jokes or meaningful milestones, your bracelets are sure to be special.

Pattern: Charmed Bracelets

Materials needed: Several skeins of embroidery thread, various charms, jump rings, jewelry pliers (optional), scissors, clipboard or tape.

Instructions:

1. Choose a bracelet pattern and follow the instructions to create the bracelet base.

2. Once the bracelet is complete, use jump rings and jewelry pliers to attach the charms to the bracelet.

3. You can add charms directly to strands of embroidery thread or attach them to jump rings and then attach the jump rings to the bracelet.

4. Experiment with different placements and combinations of charms to create a bracelet that reflects the unique bond between you and your friends.

5. Once all the charms are attached, tie a knot at the end to tie the strands together, leaving a small loop for fastening.

Conclusion

As we conclude our journey through the world of friendship bracelet designs, remember that the true beauty of these creations lies not only in their aesthetic appeal, but also in the love and memories they represent. Whether you're making bracelets for yourself or sharing them with friends, let each knot tied be a testament to the lasting friendships that enrich our lives.

Made in the USA
Las Vegas, NV
05 October 2024

96324636R40030